The New Life

The Start of Something Wonderful

DAVE WILLIAMS

THE NEW LIFE…

The Start of Something Wonderful

Unless otherwise noted, all Scripture quotations are taken from the *King James Version* of the Bible.

Scripture quotations marked NLT are taken from the *Holy Bible, New Living Translation*, copyright © 1996, 2004, 2007 by Tyndale House Foundation. Used by permission of Tyndale House Publishers, Inc., Carol Stream, Illinois 60188. All rights reserved.

Scripture quotations marked CEV are taken from the *Contemporary English Version*® Copyright © 1995 American Bible Society. All rights reserved.

Scripture quotations marked MSG are taken from *The Message*. Copyright © 1993, 1994, 1995, 1996, 2000, 2001, 2002. Used by permission of NavPress Publishing Group.

Copyright © 1983 by David R. Williams
Thirty first Printing 2017

Paperback Edition: ISBN 978-0-938020-03-5
Ebook Edition: ISBN 978-1-62985-033-7

Cover by Lindsay Allison & Kristy Grundner

DECAPOLIS
PUBLISHING
Lansing, MI
DecapolisPublishing.com

Printed in the United States of America

Books by Dave Williams*

ABCs of Success and Happiness
The Art of Pacesetting Leadership†
Angels: They Are Watching You!
Beatitudes: Success 101
The Beauty of Holiness
Coming into the Wealthy Place†
The Desires of Your Heart
Developing the Spirit of a Conqueror
Elite Prayer Warriors
Emerging Leaders
Filled
Genuine Prosperity
Gifts that Shape Your Life & Change Your World
Grief and Mourning
Have You Heard from the Lord Lately?
How to be a High Performance Believer
How to Help Your Pastor Succeed†
The Imposter†
The Jezebel Spirit
Miracle Breakthrough Power of the First Fruit†
The Miracle of Faith Goals†
The New Life...The Start of Something Wonderful†
The Pastor's Pay
The Presence of God
Private Garden†
Radical Fasting†
Radical Forgiveness
Radical Healing
Regaining Your Spiritual Momentum
The Road to Radical Riches†
The Secret of Power With God
Seven Sign Posts on the Road to Spiritual Maturity
Skill for Battle†
The Spirit of Antagonism†
Supernatural Gifts of the Holy Spirit
Toxic Committees & Venomous Boards†
The World Beyond†
Your Pastor: A Key to Your Personal Wealth
Your Spectacular Mind†

*Available at DecapolisPublishing.com
† Ebook versions available

Table of Contents

Welcome to the New Life 7

First Word 12

1: Take a Public Stand for Jesus 15

2: Never Look Back to the Old Life 17

3: Get Baptized in Water 19

4: Begin a Regular Prayer Life 21

5: Read Your Bible Daily 28

6: Renounce Your Old Life of Sin 33

7: Share Christ with Others 35

8: Become Filled with the Holy Spirit 38

9: Use Your Prayer Language Daily 40

10: Get Rid of "Old Life" Reminders 42

11: Choose the Right Friends 44

12: Deal Effectively with Temptation 47

13: Make Your Faith Grow 50

14: Grow Spiritually and Produce Fruit 53

15: Join a Christ-Centered Church 58

16: Be Faithful in Giving to God 62

17: Use Your Talents for God 73

18: Prepare for Christ's Return 74

19: Be a Good Citizen 77

20: Get Along with Others 79

21: Beware of Common Causes of Failure 82

22: Beware of False Doctrine 85

23: Take Care of Your Body 87

24: Press Toward these Goals 89

25: Seek to Develop these Traits 90

26: Read Uplifting Material 91

Special Projects 93

Conclusion 94

God has promised to forgive you, if you tell him about your sin.

WELCOME TO
THE NEW LIFE

I want to congratulate you on your commitment to follow Jesus. Right now angels are rejoicing over your decision, and the devil is trembling. You see, when you took a stand for God, the devil knew he lost—permanently—in your life. You are a child of God today with much greater power than all of hell's forces. You have a new life!

> **"But as many as received him [Jesus], to them gave he power to become the sons [and daughters] of God, even to them that believe on his name..."**
>
> **John 1:12 (brackets added)**

Even the most wicked person on earth becomes a precious and powerful child of God the very instant he or she receives Jesus Christ. You have a call and a destiny now, regardless of how "bad" you were, or how "good" you were. We all come to God in the same way.

Jesus said:

> …I am the way, the truth, and the life: no man cometh unto the Father, but by me.
>
> **John 14:6b**

You are a new person today. You have a brand new life! All your sins have been forgiven.

USE YOUR NEW POWER

Now, I know the devil will whisper in your mind that it didn't work for you. Then he will remind you of all the wrong you've ever done. But today, you can use your new power from God to tell Satan to, *"Scram! Get out and stay out!"* Tell the devil, *"I'm a new person. My past is forgiven and I'm a powerful child of God. By the authority of Jesus, I command you, devil, to go!"*

And, he must go! Look at this Scripture, and think about the magnitude of God's promise to YOU!

> **Surrender to God! Resist the devil, and he will run from you.**
>
> **James 4:7 CEV**

I want to encourage you to grow strong in your faith and in your new life. You have a destiny to make a difference in this world for God. And, just as your physical body has certain needs, so do your soul and spirit.

HOW I LEARNED TO GROW IN GOD

These principles will help you in your new life as a born-again Christian. They are the ones I used, and I know they will help you along the way.

1. A Proper Diet

In order to grow strong, you need good nutrition. Your spirit—the part of you that God communicates with—needs good nutrition too. Where do you find spiritual food? You find it in the Bible. In Matthew 11:29, Jesus said, "Learn of me." In John 6:63, he also said, "...the words that I speak to you, they are spirit, and they are life." The Bible is your spiritual food.

Read the Gospels of Matthew, Mark, Luke, and John. Learn about Jesus. Read as much as you can every day, and God will open fresh truths to your heart that will help you become successful in every area of your life. Just as your body needs daily food, so does your spirit. God will show you, through the Holy Spirit, important things you need to know each day.

Seek out other Christians. You'll need positive, encouraging associations to help feed your spirit. A nutritious spiritual diet is very important to your success, and it's God's plan for you to form close connections with other believers.

2. Exercise

Just as you need to exercise a muscle to make it grow, you need to exercise—or practice—being a Christian in order to grow spiritually.

It helps to be involved with other solid believers. They will help you learn how to share your faith, how to walk in victory, how to pray for others, and even how to cast out demons! If you don't have a church home yet, search for one that believes the Bible and believes in the miracle-working power of God that is at work in the world today.

3. Proper Rest

Yes, I mean rest. What do I mean by rest? Simply this: There comes a time when we must leave our future in the hands of

God. We cannot rest if we are filled with fear, worry, and anxiety about tomorrow.

Talk to God. Tell him your cares, then cast them all upon him. God will be faithful to take care of you. You cannot rest if you are filled with fear, worry, and anxiety about tomorrow.

> **God cares for you, so turn all your worries over to him.**
>
> 1 Peter 5:7 CEV

> **There remaineth therefore a rest to the people of God.**
>
> Hebrews 4:9

YOU ARE A WINNER

God called you to be a winner. You are more than a conqueror through Jesus Christ. You are a person with a destiny.

Now, let me share another thing: God knows it takes a while to practice being a champion believer. Sometimes we "stumble" or "slip." I sure did. But, in his kindness, God gave us several promises just in case we slip in our walk with him.

First, he assures us that he does not condemn us.

> **There is therefore now no condemnation to them which are in Christ Jesus....**
>
> Romans 8:1a

Second, God has promised to forgive you if you tell him about your sin. If you confess your wrongdoings to God, he will forgive you and help you to go on from there. This way, the devil can't succeed when he whispers, "You've sinned...you're all mine now." No! You belong to God now.

> **But if we confess our sins to God, he can always be trusted to forgive us and take our sins away.**
>
> 1 John 1:9 CEV

HOW THIS BOOK WILL HELP YOU

This book will help you learn more about Jesus. It will teach you how to talk with him, how to read his Word, the Bible, how to introduce him to your friends, and much more! You will want to look up all the suggested Scripture meditations in your Bible. Doing this will help you learn where the various books of the Bible are located and will teach you the importance of referring to the "Word" in all situations of life. Studying God's Word will be a thrilling, heart-stirring experience for you.

After you have completed reading this book and looking up all the prescribed Scripture meditations, ask your pastor, or a trusted Christian leader, to fill out the certificate of completion found in the back of this book. You may want to make notes in the margins of your certificate, such as the day you were baptized in water, the day you were filled with the Holy Spirit, and other significant spiritual events in your life. These notes will remind you of your commitment to Jesus and of his promises to you. God bless you as you...

> **Study to shew thyself approved unto God, a workman that needeth not to be ashamed.**
>
> **2 Timothy 2:15**

And thanks for letting me share these thoughts with you. I care about you; God cares about you. I pray God's richest blessings on your life.

Your friend in Jesus,

Dave Williams

Dave Williams, D. Min.

FIRST WORD

A young man named Reggie had the dream of becoming a famous rock musician. He worked with several well-known rock groups and famous musicians, and he gradually climbed the ladder of success and found fame and fortune.

With several gold records to his credit, Reggie had reached the top. He saw his dreams come true, yet there still remained an unexplainable emptiness in his life. There was no genuine peace, no joy, and no love.

Surrounding this successful writer of rock music were all the things he had dreamed about: fame, money, travel, women, popularity, and excitement.

But something was drastically wrong. Reggie saw many of his "successful" friends suffer the consequences of drug and alcohol abuse and die from overdoses. Some committed suicide. Others turned to homosexuality and other forms of sexual debasement in order to experience new highs for their fleshly appetites.

WHAT WAS WRONG?

Disillusioned with life, unfulfilled by success, running away from reality, Reggie turned on the television in his hotel room one night after returning from a concert. On the screen he saw the Reverend Billy Graham!

"You've run far enough," Billy's voice rang out, "You've come to the end of the road. It's time to turn your life over to Jesus Christ—completely and wholeheartedly!"

Tears welled up in Reggie's eyes as he experienced God's call in his heart. He knelt by the television and prayed, "Oh God, please be merciful to me, a sinner. I'm sorry for the wrong I have done. I believe you died on the cross for me, and I believe you were raised from the dead. Please come into my heart, Jesus, and change me."

That night Reggie became a new creation. He began a new life. Now instead of having selfish desires, carnal dreams and plans, he wanted to give all his dreams and plans to Jesus Christ. In return, the Lord gave Reggie a new dream, a new vision, a new desire, and a new life!

Now Reggie travels the country telling people about Jesus. He has written a book, made Gospel music albums, and appeared on national television programs giving his testimony of how Jesus Christ changed his life and made him brand new.

Reggie made the decision to follow Jesus 100 percent—not 80 percent, or 75 percent—but **100 percent**. And Jesus gave him new desires. Now the desire to sin was gone. Oh yes, there were still temptations, but the root desire to sin was gone. Now his greatest desire was to please the Master. He had found that the only true success—eternal success—is found in a man named **Jesus Christ, the Son of God**.

Today, Reggie has real peace, real joy, real love, and real fulfillment...not a phony substitute. Why? Because he has been given a new life! The old things are passed away.

When you prayed and asked Jesus to come into your life, he gave you a new life too...and a brand new start.

Are you ready? Let's get started on our journey to becoming a rock-solid disciple of Jesus Christ.

> **Therefore if any man be in Christ, he is a new creature: old things are passed away; behold, all things are become new.**
>
> **2 Corinthians 5:17**

In order to truly make Jesus Christ the Lord of your life as Reggie did, there are certain things you will want to do after receiving the new life. These things will help you become a victorious, successful Christian—a "one hundred percenter."

CHAPTER 1

TAKE A PUBLIC STAND FOR JESUS

Scripture Meditations:

☐ *Matthew 10:32–33*   ☐ *2 Timothy 2:12*
☐ *Luke 12:8–9*

Let others know immediately that you have decided to follow Jesus. The longer you wait, the more difficult it will become. People may persecute you, ridicule you, and criticize you. Be prepared for it!

Scripture Meditations:

☐ *2 Timothy 3:12*   ☐ *Matthew 5:10–12*

The reason for this is because you have become a prime target for the devil. He wants to rob you of your victory in Christ. He hates to see people happily rejoicing in Jesus, so he stirs up trouble to try to rob you.

Scripture Meditations:

☐ *John 10:10*   ☐ *Ephesians 6:10–11*
☐ *1 Peter 5:8*

As a Christian, you should pray for the people who criticize you. Ask God to bless them and help them see the "light." Ask God to convict them of their sins, that they too will come to know the joy of following Christ.

Scripture Meditations:

☐ *Matthew 5:44–47*   ☐ *Romans 12:14*

CHAPTER 2

NEVER LOOK BACK
TO THE OLD LIFE

Keep your eyes on Jesus, not on people, projects, programs, or things. People will fail. They are not perfect. We all have certain weaknesses and others cannot live up to our expectations all of the time. That's why you must always look to Jesus.

You will probably go through a faultfinding period in your Christian experience. Most Christians do. This is where the devil shows you everything wrong in everybody else. He will show you the pastor's shortcomings. He will show you other people's faults and weaknesses. If you listen to him you might even quit your church and go somewhere else, only to discover the same situation all over again.

Or, you may try to grow spiritually by watching religious shows on television or by listening to audio teachings. You might not realize that, though most of those programs are good, they cannot substitute for God's plan for your growth, which is to be in a church.

> [11] Now these are the gifts Christ gave to the church: the apostles, the prophets, the evangelists, and the pastors and teachers.
>
> [12] Their responsibility is to equip God's people to do his work and build up the church, the body of Christ.
>
> **Ephesians 4:11–12 NLT**

It's sad to say, but most people never grow beyond the "faultfinding" stage of development.

Keep your eyes on Christ. Don't ever look back to the old life. According to the Bible, you now are in a race. Run the race to win, not come in second or third. Run to win!

> Don't you realize that in a race everyone runs, but only one person gets the prize? So run to win!
>
> **1 Corinthians 9:24 NLT**

Don't be satisfied with a mediocre, lukewarm life. Go all out—victory or death! Burn all the bridges behind you and move ahead with Jesus Christ!

Scripture Meditations:

☐ *Revelation 3:15–16*   ☐ *Luke 9:62*

CHAPTER

GET BAPTIZED
IN WATER

You should get baptized in water at your first opportunity. Don't put it off. If you were baptized as a baby, or before you were genuinely converted to Christ, it doesn't count. Taking the step to get baptized in water is an outward sign of your true belief. It means you are openly confessing you are now dead to the old life and alive to your new life through Jesus Christ.

> He that believeth and is baptized shall be saved; but he that believeth not shall be damned.
>
> **Mark 16:16**

> ³ Know ye not, that so many of us as were baptized into Jesus Christ were baptized into his death?
>
> ⁴ Therefore we are buried with him by baptism into death: that like as Christ was raised up from the dead by the glory of the Father, even so we also should walk in newness of life.
>
> ⁵ For if we have been planted together in the likeness of his death, we shall be also in the likeness of his resurrection:

⁶ Knowing this, that our old man is crucified with him, that the body of sin might be destroyed, that henceforth we should not serve sin.

⁷ For he that is dead is freed from sin.

⁸ Now if we be dead with Christ, we believe that we shall also live with him:

⁹ Knowing that Christ being raised from the dead dieth no more; death hath no more dominion over him.

Romans 6:3–9

Scripture Meditations:

- ☐ *Matthew 3:6*
- ☐ *Acts 8:12*
- ☐ *Acts 9:18*
- ☐ *Acts 16:33*
- ☐ *Acts 22:16*
- ☐ *Matthew 28:19*
- ☐ *Acts 2:38*
- ☐ *Acts 8:36–39*
- ☐ *Acts 16:15*
- ☐ *Acts 18:8*
- ☐ *Romans 6:3–9*

4
CHAPTER

BEGIN A REGULAR PRAYER LIFE

This is perhaps one of the most exciting areas of our Christian walk. We have the unique privilege of communicating with our Creator. That's really what prayer is—communion with God. Prayer will help you find the perfect will of God for your life as you begin to seek him on a daily basis.

Prayer is one area where Satan will try to attack you the hardest. It's because he knows that through faith-filled prayer, great advances are wrought in the Kingdom of God, and great damage is brought to his own miserable kingdom of darkness.

Prayer is the source of the Christian's power. It should be a daily habit. Start out by regularly setting aside 15 minutes each day for prayer. As you grow in the Lord, you will have more to pray about and will want to spend even more time talking with your Heavenly Father. Some Christians spend one or two hours a day in prayer. Of course, the amount of time isn't nearly as important as the quality of time you spend. Some people can pray for 15 minutes in faith and accomplish more than a person who spends five hours in prayer with no faith. Make sure your prayers are filled with faith, based upon God's promises as found in the Holy Bible.

DIFFERENT KINDS OF PRAYER

There are different kinds of prayer for different situations and circumstances. Let's look at some of them.

1. Prayer of confession

This is the kind of prayer you pray when you have sinned under a sudden temptation. Simply tell the Lord what it is you have done and ask him to forgive you. He will forgive you and it will be as though you had never sinned at all!

> If we confess our sins, he is faithful and just
> to forgive us our sins, and to cleanse us from all
> unrighteousness.
>
> **1 John 1:9**

> Indeed, the Lord will give justice to his people,
> and he will change his mind about his servants, when
> he sees their strength is gone and no one is left, slave
> or free.
>
> **Deuteronomy 32:36 NLT**

2. Prayer of petition

This is the type of prayer you pray when you desire something from the Lord. It can be just a simple request. Use your own words and talk to the Lord like he is your best friend who is right there in the room with you. He *is* your best friend, and he is right there with you every moment.

Scripture Meditations:

☐ *Mark 11:24*   ☐ *Matthew 21:22*

3. Prayer of worship and praise

This is the kind of prayer where you simply praise and thank the Lord. You don't ask him for anything, only tell him how much you love and appreciate him. Thank God and adore him for who he is and all he has done for you. Thank God in advance for answering your prayers. This is one of the most powerful forms of prayer!

Scripture Meditations:

☐ *Luke 24:50–53*   ☐ *Acts 16:25*

4. Intercessory prayer

This is the kind of prayer you pray when you are approaching God on behalf of another person. For example, you may intercede for your family members, your friends, your pastor, the president, the governor, the mayor, service men and women, etc.

Scripture Meditation:

☐ *1 Timothy 2:1–2*

5. United prayer

This is when two or more believers pray together. This is a dynamic and powerful form of prayer.

> **Again I say unto you, That if two of you shall agree on earth as touching any thing that they shall ask, it shall be done for them of my Father which is in heaven.**
>
> **Matthew 18:19**

> [24] **And when they heard that, they lifted up their voice to God with one accord, and said, Lord, thou art God, which hast made heaven, and earth, and the sea, and all that in them is:**

²⁹ And now, Lord, behold their threatenings: and grant unto thy servants, that with all boldness they may speak thy word,

³⁰ By stretching forth thine hand to heal; and that signs and wonders may be done by the name of thy holy child Jesus.

³¹ And when they had prayed, the place was shaken where they were assembled together; and they were all filled with the Holy Ghost, and they spake the word of God with boldness.

Acts 4: 24, 29–31

Scripture Meditations:

☐ *Matthew 7:7–8*

☐ *John 16:23–24*

☐ *Romans 8:26*

☐ *Acts 13:1–4*

☐ *2 Chronicles 20:17–22*

☐ *Psalm 37:5*

☐ *Luke 11:5–13*

☐ *1 Peter 3:12*

☐ *1 John 5:14*

☐ *John 15:7*

☐ *Matthew 18:18–20*

☐ *Jude 1:20*

☐ *Luke 24:52–53*

☐ *Acts 1:14*

☐ *Matthew 7:7–11*

☐ *James 5:17–18*

☐ *1 Thessalonians 5:16–18*

☐ *1 Corinthians 14:14–15*

☐ *Philippians 4:6*

☐ *John 14:14*

☐ *Matthew 21:22*

☐ *Acts 16:22–25*

☐ *Acts 4:31*

☐ *1 Peter 5:7*

☐ *James 5:13–16*

☐ *Jeremiah 29:12–13*

☐ *Mark 11:23–26*

☐ *Ephesians 5:20*

☐ *Ephesians 6:18*

☐ *Luke 22:42*

☐ *2 Chronicles 20:15*

☐ *Matthew 6:5–13*

☐ *1 Timothy 2:8*

☐ *Mark 13:33*

You will never be able to find the time to pray. You must make the time to pray. Almost immediately the enemy attacks the new believer's prayer life. He may try to inject obscene thoughts into your mind and make you think they are yours, in hopes of causing you to feel guilty and ashamed and unable to pray effectively. Or, he will try to get you thinking about all the work around the house that needs to be done so you can't concentrate on praying. But remember this: More can be accomplished in three minutes of prayer than in three hours of hard work! Of course there must be a good balance, but prayer—your time of intimate conversation with God—is extremely important to your own spiritual health, growth, and stability. Make prayer a way of life. Jesus did!

ENEMIES OF ANSWERED PRAYER

The devil doesn't want your prayers to be answered. Satan knows that when your prayers are answered, God's Kingdom moves forward while destruction is brought to his kingdom of darkness. Therefore, he sends out many enemies to hinder your prayers. It is important to recognize these enemies in order to eliminate them.

1. An impure heart

The Lord said he will not listen to you if you ignore iniquity (sin) in your heart. The solution to this problem is to put Jesus Christ first in your life. Let God's Word become your authority. When you confess your sin to God and repent of that sin, you are cleansed of all unrighteousness. Your heart is made pure by the Blood of Jesus Christ. God will then listen because the Blood of his Son has made your heart pure.

2. Wrong motives

A young man prayed, "Oh, Lord, please send me a new Corvette sports car. The only reason I want it, Lord, is so I can pick up kids and take them to Sunday school." Yeah, right! Check your motives carefully when asking God for something.

3. Failing to praise God

Learn the secret of praising God in all situations, and many prayer enemies will automatically be eliminated.

4. Poor human relations

You must forgive others if you want to receive answers to your prayers.

5. Praying against the will of God

This means asking God in prayer for something that is not part of his plan for your life. You must seek God in prayer to reveal his plans and purposes for your life, and then keep your focus on those things.

6. Negative praying

Don't tell God how rotten you are. He knows everything about you already! He considered you worthy enough to send his only Son, Jesus, to die on the cross for you. Confess your sins quickly, and then forget about them! Center your attention on Jesus and his strength, not on your weaknesses. Negative prayers get negative results.

7. Failing to be honest with God

You must worship God in Spirit and in truth. Be honest with God. He knows what is in your heart already, and he can't be tricked.

8. Failing to get quiet before the Lord

There are many spiritual motor mouths today. They can talk for six hours about nothing! Get quiet before the Lord so you can hear his voice speak to your heart.

9. Lack of persistence

You must keep claiming the promises found in God's Word if you are to succeed.

10. Lack of honest desires

You must really desire the answer to your prayer. For example, some people pray for healing, but deep down in their hearts they really desire to be sick so that they can get sympathy from others.

11. Failing to see the answer in your mind and heart

When you pray, make sure you are picturing the answer with your "eye" of faith.

12. Failing to believe the answer is on the way

God hears and answers every prayer as we abide in him and his Word abides in us.

Resist these prayer enemies, submit yourself to God, and watch your prayer life perk up!

Scripture Meditations:

☐ *1 John 5:14*　　　　☐ *Psalm 81:13*
☐ *James 4:3*　　　　　☐ *Hebrews 10:23*
☐ *John 4:24*　　　　　☐ *Matthew 18:19*
☐ *Isaiah 30:15*　　　　☐ *John 15:7*
☐ *Psalm 66:18*　　　　☐ *Psalm 46:10*
☐ *Psalm 150:6*　　　　☐ *Mark 11:24*
☐ *Mark 11:26*　　　　 ☐ *Psalm 37:4*
☐ *1 Peter 3:7*

CHAPTER 5

READ YOUR BIBLE DAILY

The Bible is God's letter to you. When you receive a letter in the mail you read it, don't you? Well, God has sent you a letter. The Bible is a list of all your assets in Christ. When you accepted Jesus Christ into your heart and life, you became a joint heir with him. Read the Bible to find out all you inherited when you started this new life.

WHY READ THE BIBLE?

> ¹⁶ All scripture is given by inspiration of God, and is profitable for doctrine, for reproof, for correction, for instruction in righteousness:
>
> ¹⁷ That the man of God may be perfect, thoroughly furnished unto all good works.
>
> 2 Timothy 3:16–17

1. It teaches you doctrine

Reading the Bible gives you guidance and shows you the right path to walk.

2. It gives you reproof

This means that it shows when you are getting off the right path—the Bible gives you direction.

3. It gives you correction

Reading the Bible tells you how to correct your course; how you can get back on the right path.

4. It gives you God's instructions

This means that it shows you how to stay on the right path.

Scripture Meditations:

- ☐ *Acts 20:32*
- ☐ *Hebrews 4:12*
- ☐ *John 15:7*
- ☐ *1 Thessalonians 2:13*
- ☐ *Ezra 7:10*
- ☐ *Isaiah 55:10–11*
- ☐ *John 8:31–32*

> **This book of the law shall not depart out of thy mouth; but thou shalt meditate therein day and night, that thou mayest observe to do according to all that is written therein: for then thou shalt make thy way prosperous, and then thou shalt have good success.**
>
> **Joshua 1:8**

The Word of God will provide genuine guidance for your life. It is the primary way that God guides his people.

> **Thy word is a lamp unto my feet, and a light unto my path.**
>
> **Psalm 119:105**

God's Word is to be used in your spiritual warfare against the devil. Read Matthew 4:1–11 and Ephesians 6:10–17 for further evidence of the benefits of using the Bible to strengthen your Christian walk.

Get to know God better by reading his Word. Read it and study it daily.

HOW TO READ THE BIBLE

1. Find a quiet place

This may be difficult but it can be done. You may have to get up an hour earlier or find yourself a spot in the basement or the attic, but you can do it...if you really want to!

2. Set a regular time

Human beings are creatures of habit. If you work various shifts, you'll not be able to have a definite time, but you could set aside the first hour of each day for Bible reading and prayer.

3. Read prayerfully

Ask God questions as you read. Ask the Holy Spirit to give you understanding of the Word and to teach you some great, practical truths that you can apply to your personal life.

4. Read and expect God to show you something wonderful

It's easier to read your Bible when you really expect God to speak to you through it.

5. Read as if God were speaking directly to you

God's Word cannot lie. The prophets wrote it as the Holy Spirit moved upon them. Read the Bible as if it were written especially for you. Remember that the Bible is God's love letter to you!

[20] Knowing this first, that no prophecy of the scripture is of any private interpretation.

²¹ For the prophecy came not in old time by the will of man: but holy men of God spake as they were moved by the Holy Ghost.

2 Peter 1:20–21

6. Have a notebook handy

You will want to write down the things God reveals to you as you read your Bible.

7. Use colored pencils or highlighters as you read

You will want to make notes in your Bible and mark certain passages that really speak to you.

SATAN'S ATTACKS

Satan is God's enemy. He is also your enemy. He will subtly attack the Scriptures to make you doubt the integrity of your Heavenly Father. On television and in the movies, Satan has used ungodly producers and comedians to attack the Bible. You should be very selective in your entertainment choices so that seeds of doubt are not sown in your mind regarding God's Word.

SOME EXCUSES SATAN WILL GIVE YOU TO NOT READ THE BIBLE

1. I don't have the time.

2. I'm too tired.

3. I can't fit it into my tight schedule.

4. Every time I read it I get sleepy.

5. I can't remember what I read anyway.

6. I don't get anything out of it.

7. I don't understand it.

8. My spouse calls me a fanatic when I read it.

9. It offends people.

10. People will say I'm crazy if I read that book.

11. I'm ashamed of it.

12. It's boring.

Yes, Satan will whisper excuses like these in your ear. There are many excuses you can find for not reading the Bible. Resist these excuses and make Bible reading of paramount importance in your life.

CHAPTER

RENOUNCE YOUR OLD LIFE OF SIN

WHAT IS SIN?

- To miss the mark of the standard
- A lapse or deviation from truth and uprightness
- A transgression
- Disobedience
- Falling short of your duty
- Actions contrary to the law

Humans are sinners for two reasons. First, we are sinners by nature, inherited from Adam. Secondly, humans are sinners by deliberate choice.

Sin loves to get a grip on you and hold you in bondage. Sin doesn't like to let go of you once it has you in its grip. If it weren't for a Holy God who provided a remedy for sin, we would all be lost and on a journey to hell.

For God was in Christ, reconciling the world to himself, no longer counting people's sins against

them. And he gave us this wonderful message of reconciliation.

2 Corinthians 5:19 NLT

Scripture Meditations:

- ☐ *Romans 5:15–20*
- ☐ *Colossians 2:13*
- ☐ *James 5:16*
- ☐ *Galatians 3:19*
- ☐ *Matthew 18:15, 21–35*
- ☐ *Psalm 51:5*
- ☐ *Romans 6:23*
- ☐ *Ephesians 1:7*
- ☐ *Galatians 6:1*
- ☐ *Romans 11:11*
- ☐ *Romans 3:9–20*
- ☐ *Isaiah 64:6*

JUMPING INTO THE CHASM

It is not how many sins we have committed that separates us from God. It is the fact that we have sinned and continue to sin. Regardless of how hard we try to be good, we cannot be good enough. We cannot earn salvation or be saved by our own merits.

For example, suppose three men try to jump across a chasm fifteen feet wide. To fail would be sure death. The first man tries hard, but he jumps only six feet and falls. The second man is more successful. He jumps ten feet, but he also falls. The third man jumps fourteen feet! However, he still suffers the same end as the first two. It makes no difference how close they came to jumping the chasm; the end result is they all died.

It is the same when it comes to dealing with your sins. Salvation is offered to you as a free gift. Forgiveness comes from believing that Jesus Christ died to pay the price for your sins. No person is too great a sinner to be saved!

Scripture Meditations:

- ☐ *Romans 6:23*
- ☐ *Isaiah 1:18*

CHAPTER 7

SHARE CHRIST WITH OTHERS

Witnessing means to tell others what you know about Christ. You don't have to be a Bible scholar or expert to share Christ with others. But you must know Jesus in order to introduce him to others.

HOW TO WITNESS

1. Prepare your heart through prayer

The more you pray and commune with the Father, the more effective you will become and the more power you will have.

2. Do not argue with people

Present Christ as a person, not as a religion.

3. Helpful Scriptures for you to share
   a. Romans 3:23 describes the problem
   b. Romans 6:23 tells the penalty
   c. Acts 3:19 gives the solution

d. John 1:12 says you must receive Christ as a personal choice

e. Revelation 3:20 tells that Christ is waiting and knocking, longing to come into your life if you will open the door to your heart.

4. Pray a simple prayer of repentance with the person and ask Jesus to come into his or her heart.

Scripture Meditations:

- ☐ *Acts 1:8*
- ☐ *Acts 4:1–37*
- ☐ *Matthew 28:19–20*
- ☐ *Mark 16:15–18*
- ☐ *1 Peter 3:15*

Assignment—Answer these Questions

1. List at least one person you can witness to:

_____

_____

_____

2. How do you plan to do this?

_____

_____

_____

3. What must you do before leading others to Christ (Matthew 4:19)?

_____

_____

_____

What did God want Paul to do since he was to
be a witness for God (Acts 22:14–15)?

_____

_____

_____

4. How does a person acknowledge Christ as Lord
   in his or her life (Romans 12:1–2)?

_____

_____

_____

5. What may cause people to ask about your
   relationship to Christ (Matthew 5:16)?

_____

_____

_____

6. What should you tell others (Acts 4:20)?

_____

_____

_____

7. What should characterize your conversation
   (Colossians 4:5–6)?

_____

_____

_____

CHAPTER 8

BECOME FILLED WITH THE HOLY SPIRIT

Now that you are a born-again Christian, there is another experience you can have with God. It is called the baptism in the Holy Spirit. It is an experience that is promised to all who will believe. The Holy Spirit will give you the power to do unusual things, such as speaking in other languages you have not learned. It may sound strange, but this experience will give you the ability to be a powerful witness for Christ.

Jesus taught us to ask for the Spirit. He didn't say to merely assume that the Holy Spirit has filled us upon conversion, but he said to ask:

> **If ye then, being evil, know how to give good gifts unto your children: how much more shall your heavenly Father give the Holy Spirit to them that ask him?**
>
> **Luke 11:13**

Some people are afraid to ask God for the Holy Spirit baptism with the evidence of speaking in other tongues, because they are afraid they will receive a demon. But Jesus explained carefully in the eleventh chapter of St. Luke that God, being a good God, would never allow such a thing to happen. If you ask for the Holy Spirit, do you honestly believe that a good God would allow an unclean spirit to come upon you? Of course not!

Jesus described the baptism in the Holy Spirit as rivers of living water flowing out of your belly. Strange as it may seem, people who ask God for the Holy Spirit baptism often experience a surge of excitement through their belly area as they begin to speak in other languages of praise unto God.

He that believeth on me, as the scripture hath said, out of his belly shall flow rivers of living water.

John 7:38

It's not necessary to feel this sensation before speaking in tongues, but it often comes when the Holy Spirit fills you. You may want to read my book, *Filled*, for more information on being filled with the Holy Spirit.

Scripture Meditations:

☐ *Matthew 3:16* ☐ *John 16:12–13*
☐ *Acts 2:1–4* ☐ *Acts 1:4–5*
☐ *Romans 8:26* ☐ *John 14:16–17*
☐ *John 14:17* ☐ *Acts 10:46*
☐ *Acts 8:17–18* ☐ *Mark 16:15–17*
☐ *Luke 11:13* ☐ *Acts 8:14–17*
☐ *Acts 2:4* ☐ *Acts 9:17*
☐ *Acts 19:6* ☐ *Luke 3:16*
☐ *1 Corinthians 12 & 13* ☐ *John 4:23–24*

CHAPTER

USE YOUR PRAYER LANGUAGE DAILY

When you receive the baptism in the Holy Spirit you will have the ability to pray in another language. Have you ever wanted to thank God for all he has done, but you couldn't seem to find the right words? Well, the Holy Spirit will give you the right words through a language known as "tongues." Some call it the "prayer language."

When you use your prayer language, you are bypassing your intellect and speaking right out of your spirit. We don't always know how to pray as we ought. That's why we need the help of the Holy Spirit and a prayer language.

Sometimes you may feel depressed or worried and not know why or how to deal with it. Begin to use your prayer language. You may not "feel" like using it, but do it anyway. You will be energized by the Spirit of God. It may sound foolish, but God has taken the foolish things to confound the wise.

**But the natural man receiveth not the things of
the Spirit of God: for they are foolishness unto him:**

neither can he know them, because they are spiritually discerned.

1 Corinthians 2:14

But God hath chosen the foolish things of the world to confound the wise; and God hath chosen the weak things of the world to confound the things which are mighty....

1 Corinthians 1:27

He that speaketh in an unknown tongue edifieth himself....

1 Corinthians 14:4a

The definition of the word "edify" in the Greek language means to charge up, like electricity. When you use your prayer language, you are being edified or charged with power. Use it every day whether you feel like it or not, and you will experience the ever-increasing joy of watching your prayers being answered supernaturally.

Sometimes it seems as though obstacles remain in the way of answered prayer. The answer seems just out of reach. What could be the cause of blocked answers? Could it be secret sin; secret habits; some chronic affliction? What is the answer? A prayer language provides a deep dimension of prayer that you can use when you don't know how to pray as you should or what you should pray.

As you begin to yield to the Spirit of God in your prayer life, you will begin to achieve victories that seem quite beyond your potential.

Scripture Meditations:

☐ *1 Corinthians 14:15*   ☐ *Romans 8:26*
☐ *1 Corinthians 14:2*   ☐ *Ephesians 6:18*

CHAPTER 10

GET RID OF "OLD LIFE" REMINDERS

This is very important, although some do not recognize it as such. Have you ever heard an old song and immediately were reminded of exactly what you were doing when it was popular? And have you ever experienced a depression after listening to music that brought back old memories? It is not a good practice to keep remnants of your old life around.

EXAMPLES OF THINGS TO GET RID OF

- Drug paraphernalia
- Photographs of old boyfriends, girlfriends, etc.
- Liquor
- Tobacco products
- Music CDs of a worldly nature
- Books and artifacts of an occult nature
- Pornography and other suggestive materials contrary to Christian principles

- Books of philosophy and other religions
- Any unwholesome materials that could cause you to stumble

Scripture Meditations:

☐ *2 Corinthians 5:17*   ☐ *Acts 19:18–19*

CHAPTER 11

CHOOSE THE RIGHT FRIENDS

Don't fool yourselves. Bad friends will destroy you.
1 Corinthians 15:33 CEV

As iron sharpens iron, so a friend sharpens a friend.
Proverbs 27:17 NLT

When you really become a Christian, you will no longer desire to go to the old hangouts and associate with the people you once did. Of course, this doesn't mean you should shun them or treat them with disrespect; it's just that you simply no longer need to chum with them. In fact, when you start witnessing to them about how Jesus transformed your life, your old friends will either get saved or decide they don't want you around anymore. You are now a "holy Joe" or a "holy roller" to them. They can't understand why you say, "Praise the Lord," at the strangest times. They can't figure out why you want to go to church all the time and talk about Jesus.

In the Old Testament, there is a story about King Jehoshaphat that vividly illustrates the importance of selecting good associates. Jehoshaphat was a godly king who went into a business alliance with an ungodly, unconverted king named Ahaziah. They built ships in a joint effort, and God allowed all of the ships to be sunk before ever being put to use because Jehoshaphat went into this unwholesome partnership.

> 35 While Jehoshaphat was king, he signed a peace treaty with Ahaziah the wicked king of Israel.
>
> 36 They agreed to build several seagoing ships at Ezion-Geber.
>
> 37 But the prophet Eliezer warned Jehoshaphat, "The LORD will destroy these ships because you have supported Ahaziah." The ships were wrecked and never sailed.
>
> 2 Chronicles 20:35–37 CEV

You cannot drink from the cup of the Lord and demons too.

I knew a young woman who said she had accepted Christ but refused to quit going to card parties. She deliberately threw herself into a place of compromise and temptation. The last time I saw her, she was back to drinking and running around and had no interest in the Lord at all. She claims that the "dirty devil" made her "do" it, but it wasn't the dirty devil that made her do it—it was her choice. She made herself do it!

When you become a genuine Christian, you will have an intense desire to associate with other Christians. You will want to be around people who can help you grow in faith and draw closer to Jesus Christ. You don't want to be around someone who serves the devil thereby dragging you back to your old life. That's why church fellowship is so vitally important.

Scripture Meditations:

- ☐ *Proverbs 1:10*
- ☐ *Galatians 2:4–5*
- ☐ *1 Corinthians 5:6*
- ☐ *Psalm 26:4–5*
- ☐ *Ephesians 5:3–14*
- ☐ *1 Corinthians 10:21*
- ☐ *Galatians 5:7–12*
- ☐ *Proverbs 25:26*
- ☐ *Ephesians 5:11*
- ☐ *Proverbs 24:1*
- ☐ *Proverbs 25:4–5*
- ☐ *Proverbs 12:26*
- ☐ *Proverbs 14:7*

If you choose the wrong friends and associates, they will become a snare to you—a thorn in your side. Make sure you are very selective in your friendships. Find faith-filled people who love Jesus and who love to pray. Choose to associate with people you know to be spiritual and who will be a positive influence upon your life. Where you spend eternity is too important to take a chance on making friends with people who will be open to satanic suggestions and cause you to stumble.

Don't misunderstand. You cannot isolate yourself. You must still rub shoulders with people and tell them about Jesus—just don't make a habit of "running" with them.

12

DEAL EFFECTIVELY WITH TEMPTATION

Just because you are now a born-again Christian, it doesn't mean that you will no longer be tempted. The reverse is true. Satan wants to win you back. He already controls the person who doesn't love the Lord, so he concentrates his efforts on trying to trip up Christians.

You will, at times, be tempted with certain sins of the flesh. Then there are times you will be tempted with sins of the mind such as worry and fear. You will be tempted in subtle ways. You must learn to live one day at a time without worrying about tomorrow. Discipline yourself to stay away from tempting situations. Some ex-drunkards go back to the bars just "to witness to their old friends." That's what they think, but actually it is a temptation from the enemy to get them back on his territory and into bad, old habits again. You must be wiser than that! Get yourself out of tempting situations immediately

Sometimes a young Christian will continue to go on dates with an unsaved person. They compromise their principles, guilt sets in, fellowship with God is broken, and they go back to the same old rut...and the devil has succeeded in his mission.

You are a child of God. You have a new life now. You do not have to let Satan make you a failure. You do not have to give in to temptation. Remember though, you cannot resist the devil in your own strength; you must do it in Christ's strength, claiming his Blood over your life and his strength over your whole being.

> 12 **But as many as received him, to them gave he power to become the sons of God, even to them that believe on his name:**
>
> 13 **Which were born, not of blood, nor of the will of the flesh, nor of the will of man, but of God.**
>
> **John 1:12–13**

> **Keep yourselves in the love of God, looking for the mercy of our Lord Jesus Christ unto eternal life.**
>
> **Jude 1:21**

HOW TO GAIN VICTORY OVER TEMPTATION

1. Claim your position in Christ

When you received Christ, you received authority over the devil. He doesn't have authority over you, although he'd like you to think so.

2. Decide firmly, without wavering, to walk in obedience to God and his Word

This is where many new Christians go wrong. They try to hang on to some secret sin instead of making the quality decision to "put off the old man" and let the fullness of the new life begin! Holding onto a secret sin will open the door to greater and more powerful temptations (Read Hebrews 12:1–4).

3. Actively resist the devil

4. Trust in God's sustaining power

Scripture Meditations:

- ☐ *Mark 16:17*
- ☐ *Ephesians 6:11–17*
- ☐ *Ephesians 1:1–23*
- ☐ *Jude 1:24*
- ☐ *1 Corinthians 10:13*
- ☐ *1 Samuel 15:22*

- ☐ *Luke 10:19*
- ☐ *James 1:5–8*
- ☐ *Genesis 39*
- ☐ *1 John 4:4*
- ☐ *1 John 5:1–5*
- ☐ *James 4:7*

CHAPTER 13

MAKE YOUR FAITH GROW

Here is one impossible thing: You can never please God without faith. All of God's work must be done by faith. You need to stand firm when the trials come. Your faith will always be tested to prove its authenticity.

The universe is expanding at the rate of 128,000 miles per second. Just as there is no limit to this ever-expanding universe, there is no limit to God's power for the person who is operating by faith.

There are different degrees, or measures, of faith. God gives to every person a measure of faith to start them off. But after that, it's up to you to make your faith grow. In the Bible you read about "weak" faith, "little" faith, "strong" faith, and "growing" faith.

Faith is claiming and laying hold of the thing you desire and bringing it out of the realm of the invisible and into the realm of the visible.

Faith is not hope. Hope is good, but it focuses upon the future. Faith takes what is hoped for and begins claiming it—now! The Bible says...

[1] Now faith is the substance of things hoped for, the evidence of things not seen.

[2] For by it the elders obtained a good report.

[3] Through faith we understand that the worlds were framed by the word of God, so that things which are seen were not made of things which do appear.

Hebrews 11:1–3

HOW DOES FAITH GROW?

- You must desire faith to grow.
- You must believe faith can grow.
- Let God's Word, the Bible, be your authority. Read it, study it, and meditate upon it daily. Develop a craving for the Word of God
- Put action to the Word. If it tells you to do something—do it!
- Speak the word with your mouth. Learn to speak the Word no matter what conditions look like. Walk by faith, not by sight. Say only what the Word says about any circumstance.
- Be willing to pass through a "waiting" period or "testing" period. This is the period of time between when you start believing a promise and the time when it actually becomes a reality in the visible realm.
- Exercise your faith and it will grow. Just like a muscle grows with exercise; your faith grows with the proper exercise.

And Jesus said unto them, Because of your unbelief: for verily I say unto you, If ye have faith as a grain of mustard seed, ye shall say unto this mountain, Remove hence to yonder place; and it shall remove; and nothing shall be impossible unto you.

Matthew 17:20

Scripture Meditations:

- [ ] *Mark 11:23–24*
- [ ] *2 Corinthians 1:24*
- [ ] *2 Thessalonians 1:3*
- [ ] *2 Corinthians 5:7*
- [ ] *Romans 1:5–31*
- [ ] *Luke 7:50*
- [ ] *Romans 3:3–4*
- [ ] *Luke 5:17–26*
- [ ] *1 Peter 1:7*
- [ ] *Romans 3:22–31*
- [ ] *Hebrews 11:1–40*
- [ ] *Romans 12:3*
- [ ] *Ephesians 3:12*
- [ ] *Mark 10:46–52*
- [ ] *Psalm 37:7*
- [ ] *Luke 7:1–10*
- [ ] *James 1:1–4*
- [ ] *Mark 6:4–6*

14

GROW SPIRITUALLY AND PRODUCE FRUIT

Nothing in life is static. Nothing remains unchanged. Everything, from the tiniest cell to the most complex creation, has an urge for a fuller, more mature life. If you do not want to grow—to mature—it is indeed a sad situation. Yet, we see Christians who have been saved for years but have never developed beyond spiritual "babyhood." This shouldn't happen.

God gave us his Word (the Bible) and the ability to communicate with him (prayer) in order that we might grow to maturity. The only thing that will prevent you from growing up spiritually is to refuse to yield to the Holy Spirit that dwells in you. If you refuse to read the Bible, or if you refuse to pray, or you refuse to fellowship with other Christians regularly, you will not grow but will remain spiritually immature. It's not difficult to recognize a twenty-year-old "baby."

You can grow as quickly or as slowly as you desire. You can go as far with God as you want. God is willing to bring you into a deep, fruitful, meaningful relationship, but you must crave spiritual things. You must want spiritual things more than your next breath.

A time will come when the excitement of the new life will wear off. You will not feel as full of enthusiasm as you did at the start. That's the time to make the decision to seek God through his Word and prayer—regardless of how you feel. Feelings have nothing to do with your walk with God. You will know you are growing when you begin to pray because you want to, and not because you feel like it.

THREE BASIC STAGES OF SPIRITUAL GROWTH

1. Babyhood

Babies can't do things for themselves very well. They must depend upon others. They have to be spoon-fed. Their diapers need changing once in a while. You can't get too angry with them over the little fusses they make. After all, they are just babies; they don't know any better. In the spiritual sense, it's okay to "spoon-feed" a new Christian for a couple of months, and change his "diapers" when he has an accident, but if it continues, something is wrong.

There comes a time when Christians must grow out of the stage where they have to call the pastor every day and request other people to pray for them all the time. There comes a time when a baby should learn to feed himself and change his own clothes. Babies should learn to do things for themselves and grow up into a child.

Babies are easily spoiled. They are easily irritated. They are easily distracted, easily frustrated, easily hurt. Nobody minds helping a little baby, but when it comes to spiritual things, we don't like to see babies that are satisfied with being babies forever!

2. Childhood Stage

Children are unsteady, curious and talkative. A child doesn't know any better, so he's always talking— always babbling about something (but usually nothing). A person in the childhood stage of spiritual development will most likely be a talker. He will usually talk about himself, his petty accomplishments, his plans, his projects, his interests, etc. His conversations are generally self-centered.

Another characteristic of children is they haven't yet learned good discipline. They are unreliable and spasmodic. In the spiritual sense, a "child" hasn't learned discipline of budgeting his time and money. He hasn't learned to get his life organized. Like in the natural, a spiritual child is unreliable; he's up and down, in and out, on and off. He reminds you of a roller coaster.

3. Adulthood

Here are some signs of spiritual maturity from evangelist Charles Finney's writings:

- **More implicit and universal trust in God**
- **A separation from the world and an increasing deadness to all the world has to offer**
- **Less temptation to sins of omission (example: neglect of prayer, Bible reading, etc.)**
- **A growing steadiness and intensity of zeal in promoting the cause of Christ**
- **Less self-consciousness and more Jesus-consciousness**
- **A growing deadness to the praise of men**
- **A growing warmth and sincere acceptance of the whole will of God**
- **A growing calmness and quietness under great afflictions**

- A growing patience under much provocation
- Joyfulness even when disappointments come
- Less temptation to gripe, complain, criticize, and murmur
- Less temptation to resent and retaliate when insulted, criticized, or abused
- Less temptation to dwell upon and magnify our trials and troubles
- Less anxiety about the future
- Less inclination to speak uncharitably about another individual
- A growing readiness to forgive others and forget old injuries
- An increasing naturalness in treating people kindly and praying for them
- Finding it easier and easier to make wholehearted sacrifices
- Finding yourself more and more impressed with revelations of Bible truths
- A growing jealousy for the honor of God and for the honor and purity of his Church

HOW TO GROW UP SPIRITUALLY

1. **Proper Diet**

Feed your spiritual life with the Word of God and prayer.

2. **Exercise**

Practice faith, hope, and love. Reach out to others in practical ways. Look for opportunities to reach out to others and to share your testimony.

3. Proper rest

Do not overdo it. God doesn't expect you to "burnout" or to "wear out."

> **There remaineth therefore a rest to the people of God.**
>
> **Hebrews 4:9**

Scripture Meditations

☐ *1 Corinthians 3:1–3*

☐ *Ephesians 4:8–15*

☐ *1 Corinthians 2:6*

☐ *1 Peter 2:2*

☐ *1 John 2:15–17*

☐ *John 3:1–7*

CHAPTER 15

JOIN A CHRIST-CENTERED CHURCH

The Church is the foundation of the Christian ministry. Jesus founded and endorsed the Church when he said, "I will build my Church." It is in the heart of every believer to have the feeling of belonging, and church membership is a scripturally sound approach to meeting the need to belong. Verses in the book of Acts indicate a very definite membership in the early Church.

> ¹² And by the hands of the apostles were many signs and wonders wrought among the people; (and they were all with one accord in Solomon's porch.
>
> ¹³ And of the rest durst no man join himself to them: but the people magnified them.
>
> ¹⁴ And believers were the more added to the Lord, multitudes both of men and women.)
>
> **Acts 5:12–14**

Also, by joining a church, you will become a voting member of that body and will be able to prayerfully help plan the programs offered by the church. For example, you will have a voice in business decisions the church must make, etc. If you see something wrong in your church, and you are not a voting member, it will be difficult to change it.

You will grow spiritually as you fellowship with believers of like faith. You will be a contributor to the health, growth, and stability of the church. Here is an example that illustrates the importance of fellowship: When working with charcoal briquettes, you gather them together. Once started, you can spread them out and cook a very large meal. But, you cannot cook much with one little coal. Like charcoal, as a member of a larger body of believers, you will have a greater impact.

Church membership is extremely important to your growth. Make the selection of a church the subject of much prayer. Although we are all members of one church (God's Heavenly Church), God puts us in a local assembly where we can do the most good for him. Pray and discover which local assembly you should attend.

Interesting Note

Did you know that military services staff chaplains based upon church membership? It's true. The armed forces supply so many chaplains per so many church denomination members. If your church has more members, then the military will provide more chaplains from your denomination. The more members a denomination has, the more military preachers they qualify for.

THINGS TO LOOK FOR IN A CHURCH

1. **The denomination professes that salvation is by faith in the shed Blood of Jesus Christ.**

Salvation is a work of grace, a gift from God, and cannot be obtained through human effort.

2. They believe that the Bible is the inspired Word of God, from Genesis to Revelation.

3. They believe God exists eternally in three Persons: God the Father, God the Son, and God the Holy Spirit.

This is known as the Holy Trinity—the Triune God.

4. They believe in water baptism.

5. They believe in Baptism in the Holy Spirit.

6. They are missions-minded.

Make sure your church supports missionary projects.

7. They believe in evangelism and actively participate in outreach and practice soul winning.

8. They believe in the ordinance of Holy Communion.

9. They believe in the imminent return of the Lord Jesus Christ.

BEWARE OF DENOMINATIONS THAT DENY...

1. The virgin birth of Christ.

2. The deity of Christ.

Deity means that Jesus Christ is actually God, the Second Person of the Trinity.

3. The blood atonement.

4. The death, burial, and resurrection of Jesus Christ.

5. That Christ's miracle-working power is still at work in the world today.

6. The imminent return of Jesus Christ.

7. The inspired, infallible Word of God—the Holy Bible.

8. That there is everlasting punishment for the unsaved.

Ministers who deny any of these cardinal doctrines of the Christian faith are not ministers of God, but of Satan!

Scripture Meditations:

- ☐ *Titus 3:10–11*
- ☐ *Hebrews 10:25*
- ☐ *1 Corinthians 5:2–3*
- ☐ *Acts 1:15*
- ☐ *Acts 4:4*
- ☐ *Acts 2:41*
- ☐ *2 Corinthians 11:14*
- ☐ *Philippians 3:18*
- ☐ *2 Peter 2*
- ☐ *Galatians 1:7–9*
- ☐ *1 Timothy 4:1–2*
- ☐ *Mark 12:29*
- ☐ *Philippians 2:5–11*
- ☐ *Romans 10:8–13*
- ☐ *Matthew 8:16–17*
- ☐ *Matthew 25:46*
- ☐ *Revelation 20:11–15*
- ☐ *Matthew 28:19*
- ☐ *Hebrews 1:2*
- ☐ *2 Timothy 3:15–17*
- ☐ *Revelation 19:20*
- ☐ *James 5:13–16*
- ☐ *1 Thessalonians 4:13–18*
- ☐ *John 3:3*
- ☐ *Acts 2:4*
- ☐ *Titus 2:13*
- ☐ *2 Peter 1:21*
- ☐ *Deuteronomy 6:4*
- ☐ *John 17:5*
- ☐ *John 3:16–17*
- ☐ *Acts 1:5*
- ☐ *Acts 19:1–7*
- ☐ *Romans 8:2*
- ☐ *1 Corinthians 15:51–52*

16
CHAPTER

BE FAITHFUL IN GIVING TO GOD

Some Christians wonder why they can never get ahead. They always seem to be in debt. They can't figure out why they can't seem to make ends meet. With things continually breaking down, clothes wearing out too fast, grocery prices soaring like a skyrocket, and bills coming in "past due," they just can't find any money left over to give to God.

They don't realize that not giving to God is the real root of their problem. God didn't ask us for the "leftovers." He said that if we would give to him first, he would see to it that our "barns would be filled to overflowing...."

> ⁸ Will a man rob God? Yet ye have robbed me. But ye say, Wherein have we robbed thee? In tithes and offerings.
>
> ⁹ Ye are cursed with a curse: for ye have robbed me, even this whole nation.
>
> ¹⁰ Bring ye all the tithes into the storehouse, that there may be meat in mine house, and prove me now

herewith, saith the LORD of hosts, if I will not open you the windows of heaven, and pour you out a blessing, that there shall not be room enough to receive it.

[11] And I will rebuke the devourer for your sakes, and he shall not destroy the fruits of your ground; neither shall your vine cast her fruit before the time in the field, saith the LORD of hosts.

Malachi 3:8–11

Scripture Meditations:

☐ *Proverbs 3:9–10*   ☐ *Deuteronomy 14:23*
☐ *Matthew 6:33*

TYPES OF GIVING

1. The tithe: This is ten percent of your gross income, which is to be given to God's work.

   Also set aside ten percent of your wine and olive oil, and the first-born of every cow, sheep, and goat. Take these to the place where the Lord chooses to be worshiped, and eat them there. This will teach you to always respect the Lord your God.

   Deuteronomy 14:23 CEV

If you do not put God first in your financial affairs, it is certain that you will not put God first in all the other areas of your life.

Some do not pay tithes because they contend that tithing was a practice that took place under Old Testament Law and not meant for the age of grace. It must be pointed out that grace is grace, but willful disobedience is not grace—it is disgrace. The principle of tithing was instituted before the Old Testament Law was given.

¹⁸ And Melchizedek king of Salem brought forth bread and wine: and he was the priest of the most high God.

¹⁹ And he blessed him, and said, Blessed be Abram of the most high God, possessor of heaven and earth:

²⁰ And blessed be the most high God, which hath delivered thine enemies into thy hand. And he gave him tithes of all.

Genesis 14:18–20

This rock will be your house, and I will give back to you a tenth of everything you give me.

Genesis 28:22 CEV

Moreover in the New Testament, Jesus himself placed his endorsement on the practice of tithing. Read Matthew 23:23. When the tithe is withheld, God's law of prosperity is violated, his law of blessing is cancelled, and it becomes increasingly difficult for you to balance your books.

2. The offering

This is any giving that is more than the ten percent tithe. Christians who dedicate themselves to Christ will soon give beyond the tithe. As God blesses them, they will increase their giving. Some believers give twenty percent, thirty percent, or even more of their income to God's work. And the more they increase their giving, the more God blesses them.

3. The special offering

This is when you give beyond your ability in the natural. You pledge a special offering amount that can only be fulfilled by God working through you. With the special offering, you ask God what you should commit to give, and then you trust him to provide it supernaturally. Through your faithfulness, God will use you as a channel for the special offering to flow.

Some people call this a faith promise, and many churches use this method of giving to finance missionary projects.

> [1] Now I want you to know, dear brothers and sisters, what God in his kindness has done through the churches in Macedonia.
>
> [2] They are being tested by many troubles, and they are very poor. But they are also filled with abundant joy, which has overflowed in rich generosity.
>
> [3] For I can testify that they gave not only what they could afford, but far more. And they did it of their own free will.
>
> [4] They begged us again and again for the privilege of sharing in the gift for the believers in Jerusalem.
>
> 2 Corinthians 8:1–4 NLT

Some people give only what they can afford. Others give beyond what they can afford and learn to experience God's supernatural blessings of supply.

PRINCIPLES OF GIVING

1. You must purpose in your heart to give

Don't wait for a bolt of lightning from Heaven to strike you and a thundering voice to tell you to start giving. You must purpose in your heart to do it.

2. You must give on a regular basis

Giving must become a habit, a way of life for you. The enemy will give you a great number of excuses for not giving. They will seem logical and reasonable, but don't listen to them because...

> So let's not allow ourselves to get fatigued doing good. At the right time *we will harvest a good crop if we don't give up, or quit.*
>
> Galatians 6:9 MSG (italics added)

Don't be discouraged when the times of testing come. Continue to give regularly and you will see God work miracles of provision on your behalf.

3. Giving must be done cheerfully

> Every man according as he purposeth in his heart, so let him give; not grudgingly, or of necessity: for God loveth a cheerful giver.
>
> 2 Corinthians 9:7

4. Giving should be sacrificial

> I have been paid back everything, and with interest. I am completely satisfied with the gifts that you had Epaphroditus bring me. They are like a sweet-smelling offering or like the right kind of sacrifice that pleases God.
>
> Philippians 4:18 CEV

> [41] Jesus was sitting in the temple near the offering box and watching people put in their gifts. He noticed that many rich people were giving a lot of money.
>
> [42] Finally, a poor widow came up and put in two coins that were worth only a few pennies.
>
> [43] Jesus told his disciples to gather around him. Then he said: I tell you that this poor widow has put in more than all the others.
>
> [44] Everyone else gave what they didn't need. But she is very poor and gave everything she had. Now she doesn't have a cent to live on.
>
> Mark 12:41–44 CEV

5. Giving must be generous

Read 2 Corinthians 8:7, 12, and 2 Corinthians 9:5.

Don't be selfish and eager to get rich—you will end up worse off than you can imagine.

> Proverbs 28:22 CEV

The LORD blesses everyone who freely gives....

> Proverbs 22:9a CEV

...a good person is generous and never stops giving.

> Psalm 37:21 CEV

[24] Give freely and become more wealthy; be stingy and lose everything.

[25] The generous will prosper; those who refresh others will themselves be refreshed.

> Proverbs 11:24–25 NLT

6. Giving must be done in faith and in obedience to God's Word

[8] You people are robbing me, your God. And, here you are, asking, "How are we robbing you?" You are robbing me of the offerings and of the ten percent that belongs to me.

[9] That's why your whole nation is under a curse.

[10] I am the LORD All-Powerful, and I challenge you to put me to the test. Bring the entire ten percent into the storehouse, so there will be food in my house. Then I will open the windows of heaven and flood you with blessing after blessing.

[11] I will also stop locusts from destroying your crops and keeping your vineyards from producing.

> Malachi 3:8–11 CEV

As a result of your ministry, they will give glory to God. For your generosity to them and to all believers will prove that you are obedient to the Good News of Christ.

> 2 Corinthians 9:13 NLT

7. Giving must be done for Jesus and for the Gospel's sake

> Take heed that ye do not your alms before men, to be seen of them: otherwise ye have no reward of your Father which is in heaven.
>
> Matthew 6:1

> [5] If any of you lack wisdom, let him ask of God, that giveth to all men liberally, and upbraideth not; and it shall be given him.
>
> [6] But let him ask in faith, nothing wavering. For he that wavereth is like a wave of the sea driven with the wind and tossed.
>
> [7] For let not that man think that he shall receive any thing of the Lord.
>
> [8] A double minded man is unstable in all his ways.
>
> James 1:5–8

Scripture Meditations:

☐ *2 Corinthians 9:7*   ☐ *Mark 10:29–30*

☐ *2 Corinthians 8:8*

PROMISES TO THE PERSON WHO GIVES IN FAITH

1. Prosperity for the generous

Remember, "whoever sows sparingly will also reap sparingly, and whoever sows generously will also reap generously," Read Luke 6:38; 2 Corinthians 9:6.

> [1] Shout praises to the LORD! The LORD blesses everyone who worships him and gladly obeys his teachings.
>
> [2] Their descendants will have great power in the land, because the LORD blesses all who do right.

³ They will get rich and prosper and will always be remembered for their fairness.

⁴ They will be so kind and merciful and good, that they will be a light in the dark for others who do the right thing.

⁵ Life will go well for those who freely lend and are honest in business.

⁶ They won't ever be troubled, and the kind things they do will never be forgotten.

Psalm 112:1–6 CEV

2. You are promised a thirty, sixty, or one-hundred fold return now, in this life

Where else can you find such a tremendous yield on an investment?

²⁹ And he said unto them, Verily I say unto you, There is no man that hath left house, or parents, or brethren, or wife, or children, for the kingdom of God's sake,

³⁰ Who shall not receive manifold more in this present time, and in the world to come life everlasting.

Luke 18:29–30

But he shall receive an hundredfold now in this time, houses, and brethren, and sisters, and mothers, and children, and lands, with persecutions; and in the world to come eternal life.

Mark 10:30

3. You are promised treasure in your heavenly bank account

You have a bank account in Heaven that is gaining interest every day. It's an account that no depression or recession can touch; no thief can steal from, and no corruption can destroy. You can draw from this account by faith when you have a need. Read Matthew 6:20; Philippians 4:17–19.

> ³² Fear not, little flock; for it is your Father's good pleasure to give you the kingdom.
>
> ³³ Sell that ye have, and give alms; provide yourselves bags which wax not old, a treasure in the heavens that faileth not, where no thief approacheth, neither moth corrupteth.
>
> ³⁴ For where your treasure is, there will your heart be also.
>
> Luke 12:32–34

4. You will "eat from the best of the land!"

God promises you his best when you give him your best.

> ¹⁹ If you willingly obey me, the best crops in the land will be yours.
>
> ²⁰ But if you turn against me, your enemies will kill you. I, the LORD, have spoken.
>
> Isaiah 1:19–20 CEV

> "I lifted the burden from your shoulder and took the heavy basket from your hands."
>
> Psalm 81:6 CEV

> Our LORD and our God, you are like the sun and also like a shield. You treat us with kindness and with honor, never denying any good thing to those who live right.
>
> Psalm 84:11 CEV

5. You will be blessed beyond human understanding

> I am the LORD All-Powerful, and I challenge you to put me to the test. Bring the entire ten percent into

the storehouse, so there will be food in my house.
Then I will open the windows of heaven and flood you
with blessing after blessing.

Malachi 3:10 CEV

⁹ Honor the LORD by giving him your money and
the first part of all your crops.

¹⁰ Then you will have more grain and grapes than
you will ever need.

Proverbs 3:9–10 CEV

6. God will rebuke the devourer for your sake

Things you own will for "some strange reason" seem to last
longer. For example, while others are getting only 40,000 miles
on a set of tires, you may get 80,000!

I will also stop locusts from destroying your crops
and keeping your vineyards from producing.

Malachi 3:11 CEV

7. Your needs will always be met

After the Philippians had given so that St. Paul was amply
supplied to carry on his work of promoting the Gospel, he told
them, "And my God shall supply all your need according to his
riches in glory by Christ Jesus." Even during times of trouble,
famine, and despair, the faithful, obedient giver will have
plenty to eat!

¹⁸ Those who obey the LORD are daily in his care,
and what he has given them will be theirs forever.

¹⁹ They won't be in trouble when times are bad, and
they will have plenty when food is scarce.

Psalm 37:18–19 CEV

[25] As long as I can remember, good people have never been left helpless, and their children have never gone begging for food.

[26] They gladly give and lend, and their children turn out good.

Psalm 37:25–26 CEV

17

CHAPTER

USE YOUR TALENTS FOR GOD

You are unique—one of a kind. When God made you, he threw away the blueprint. There is not another person on earth quite like you. You have special gifts and talents from God that he wants you to use for his glory.

It may be a gift of singing, or teaching, or being able to play a musical instrument. It may be the capacity to preach, or even mow lawns, wash windows, paint—whatever! But you can be sure of this: God has given you a special talent.

When you come to know Jesus Christ in a real way, you will not have a great desire to use your talents to glorify yourself. Instead, you will want to glorify Jesus with the talents God has given you.

Scripture Meditations:

☐ *Matthew 25:14–30*   ☐ *Exodus 35*

18
CHAPTER

PREPARE FOR CHRIST'S RETURN

Jesus Christ promised to return to the earth. By all indications, his return could take place any day now. Many discerning Bible scholars believe that we are now in the final hours of history. The stage is set; the conditions are right; the Scriptures that foretold of Jesus' return to earth are being fulfilled. Jesus can appear at any moment to evacuate his people from the earth just before the world's deepest hour of agony.

Many people do not understand that the second coming of Christ will occur in two distinct phases:

Phase 1—Christ comes FOR the Christians.
Phase 2—Christ comes WITH the Christians.

I believe that some of the people who are reading this book will never see death but will be translated to meet the Lord in the air at his coming. That's how close I believe we are to that day of the "Blessed Hope."

¹² Teaching us that, denying ungodliness and worldly lusts, we should live soberly, righteously, and godly, in this present world;

¹³ Looking for that blessed hope, and the glorious appearing of the great God and our Saviour Jesus Christ;

¹⁴ Who gave himself for us, that he might redeem us from all iniquity, and purify unto himself a peculiar people, zealous of good works.

Titus 2:12–14

HOW TO PREPARE TO MEET JESUS

1. By faith receive Jesus into your heart as your personal Lord and Savior

2. Walk in all the light that you have

In other words, do what you know is right, do the best you know how.

3. Develop your faith

It was by faith that Enoch was translated without ever tasting death. **He went directly to Heaven without dying!**

4. Look for Jesus' Second Coming; anticipate it every day

5. Practice evangelism

Reach out to everyone you meet with the Good News of Jesus Christ.

6. Have a missionary mind-set

7. Develop a genuine love for people

8. Avoid hypocrisy

9. Stay close to Jesus and make like-minded believers your closest associates

10. Do the Lord's work with patience and an unselfish attitude

11. Watch and pray always that you will be counted worthy to escape the coming time of trouble and to stand before Jesus with confidence

Scripture Meditations:

- ☐ *2 Corinthians 5:10*
- ☐ *Luke 21:1–38*
- ☐ *1 Timothy 4:1–2*
- ☐ *Matthew 24:1–51*
- ☐ *Romans 8:23*
- ☐ *2 Timothy 3:1–5*
- ☐ *1 Thessalonians 4:13–18*
- ☐ *1 Corinthians 15:51–52*
- ☐ *John 14:1–3*
- ☐ *Acts 1:10–11*
- ☐ *Luke 18:8*
- ☐ *Titus 2:11–13*
- ☐ *Luke 17:26–30*
- ☐ *1 John 3:3*

19
CHAPTER

BE A GOOD CITIZEN

You are now a representative of Jesus Christ. It is important that you represent him well. This means you pay your bills on time; you keep your word; you pray for our governmental officials instead of complaining about them. In other words, you decide to become a good citizen. Although this earth is not our final home, we are here now and have certain responsibilities to our fellow man and to our country.

¹ **Let every soul be subject unto the higher powers. For there is no power but of God: the powers that be are ordained of God.**

² **Whosoever therefore resisteth the power, resisteth the ordinance of God: and they that resist shall receive to themselves damnation.**

³ **For rulers are not a terror to good works, but to the evil. Wilt thou then not be afraid of the power? do that which is good, and thou shalt have praise of the same:**

⁴ **For he is the minister of God to thee for good. But if thou do that which is evil, be afraid; for he beareth**

not the sword in vain: for he is the minister of God, a revenger to execute wrath upon him that doeth evil.

⁵ Wherefore ye must needs be subject, not only for wrath, but also for conscience sake.

⁶ For this cause pay ye tribute also: for they are God's ministers, attending continually upon this very thing.

⁷ Render therefore to all their dues: tribute to whom tribute is due; custom to whom custom; fear to whom fear; honour to whom honour.

Romans 13:1–7

As God's people, we have the duty to pray for our leaders, both spiritual and political. On a daily basis we need to take authority over the powers of darkness that would seek to destroy our nation.

> We are not fighting against humans. We are fighting against forces and authorities and against rulers of darkness and powers in the spiritual world.
>
> **Ephesians 6:12 CEV**

We must bind them in the Name of Jesus!

> Verily I say unto you, Whatsoever ye shall bind on earth shall be bound in heaven: and whatsoever ye shall loose on earth shall be loosed in heaven.
>
> **Matthew 18:18**

The devil will do his best to ruin your country and your leaders, if we don't use our God-given authority over him.

20

GET ALONG WITH OTHERS

It's no easy task to get along with others, because we are all so different. We have different backgrounds, different schooling, different upbringing, and different past experiences. Our opinions vary on certain issues and we have different ideas on different subjects. It's not easy to be at peace with those who disagree with us even on minor issues.

Nonetheless, the Holy Spirit, through the writings of St. Paul, said to "...live peaceably with all men." We don't have to agree with everyone about everything, and we don't even have to respect their opinions, but we must respect them as human beings who have been created in the image and likeness of God.

GENERAL RULES FOR GETTING ALONG WITH PEOPLE

1. **Take a genuine interest in other people.**
   Read Philippians 2:20–21

2. **Never use cheap flattery to win favor.**
   Read 1 Thessalonians 2:5

> Watch out for anyone who tells lies and flatters—
> they are out to get you.
>
> **Proverbs 26:28 CEV**

3. Never rebuke an older person harshly.
   See 1 Timothy 5:1

4. Avoid foolish and stupid arguments.
   Read 2 Timothy 2:23

5. Always offer hospitality without grumbling.
   Read 1 Peter 4:9

6. Never embarrass another person for any reason

   > [4] Hanun arrested David's officials and had their
   > beards shaved off on one side of their faces. He had
   > their robes cut off just below the waist, and then he
   > sent them away.
   >
   > [5] They were terribly ashamed.
   >
   > **2 Samuel 10:4–5a CEV**

7. Let your conversation always be full of grace.
   Read Colossians 4:6 in your Bible

8. Always say "Thanks!" to anyone who has
   helped you

   > One of them, when he saw that he was healed,
   > came back to Jesus, shouting, "Praise God!"
   >
   > **Luke 17:15 NLT**

9. Appreciate other people. Focus on their
   good points

10. Don't praise or brag about yourself to others

> Don't brag about yourself—let others praise you.
>
> Proverbs 27:2 CEV

11. Always be sincere; never be phony.
    Read Romans 12:9.

12. Speak words to encourage and strengthen
    others. See Acts 15:32

13. Don't be unjustly critical of others.

> [41] You can see the speck in your friend's eye. But you don't notice the log in your own eye.
>
> [42] How can you say, "My friend, let me take the speck out of your eye," when you don't see the log in your own eye? You show-offs! First, get the log out of your own eye. Then you can see how to take the speck out of your friend's eye.
>
> Luke 6:41–42 CEV

14. Don't talk too much

> Stay away from gossips—they tell everything.
>
> Proverbs 20:19 CEV

21
CHAPTER

BEWARE OF COMMON CAUSES OF FAILURE

Here is a list of the most common causes of failure in a Christian's life:

- Lack of confidence in God and in his Word
- Not forging ahead with a whole heart but reluctantly dragging your feet
- Having a desire that is contrary to God's will
- Beginning to think about what you don't have instead of all the things you do have
- Thinking only of what you can do in your own strength instead of thinking in terms of God's unlimited supply
- Lack of perseverance during times of difficulty in your life
- Wasting a lot of time on silly magazines, television programs, etc., instead of using your time to study God's Word or listen to teaching

messages, or read books by anointed Christian teachers
- Selfishness
- Not desiring God's will above everything else in your life
- Flirting with the world and its amusements
- Pride
- Compromising your principles
- Lack of prayer, fellowship, and Bible reading
- Not sharing your faith with others who don't know Jesus
- Fear and uncertainty
- Poor choice of friends and associates
- Laziness
- Materialism
- Looking for a shortcut to spirituality
- Having a negative mind-set
- Allowing Satan to distort your concept of God
- Putting anything ahead of Jesus
- Conforming to the world's systems and philosophies
- Lack of vision and having no goals in your Christian life
- Lack of Bible knowledge, and not asking the Holy Spirit to reveal the Bible's truths to your heart
- Resentment of authority
- Lack of trust in God that he will keep you safe and meet your every need
- Not expecting the return of Jesus for his Church
- Shunning responsibility—not becoming involved in church activities, etc.

- Continuing to sin after Christ has set you free
- Expressing unbelief in your thoughts, words, and actions
- Self-deception by not being a doer of God's Word or not speaking like God speaks. In other words, speaking as though God's Word is not really true
- Criticizing a man or woman of God
- Having a hard heart toward others—particularly those who are hurting in some way
- Instead of being a diligent seeker of God, you are only a "casual inquirer"

Whenever you notice the victory being squeezed out of your Christian experience, check this list over. You will most likely see where you have been missing the mark.

22
CHAPTER

BEWARE OF FALSE DOCTRINE

There are many philosophies and religions in the world that do not believe that Jesus Christ is the only way to Heaven. There are also many teachings that might espouse a belief in Jesus Christ, but do not use God's Holy Word as a foundation. Satan continually looks for ways to lead believers astray through false teachings. It is essential that you measure everything you read, hear, or are told, against the only true standard—God's will as revealed through his Holy Word, the Bible. You will never go wrong as long as what you believe can be confirmed in God's Word.

The Bible instructs us to test the spirits to see if they are of God. Jesus said to beware of false prophets. In the Greek language, the word "beware" actually means to shun, avoid, and stay away from.

Don't dabble in things you know to be false, because little by little those lies begin to penetrate your resistance if you keep toying around with them.

> **If you stop listening to instruction, my child, you will turn your back on knowledge.**
>
> **Proverbs 19:27 NLT**

Ask your pastor if you are ever in any doubt about a teaching or a group. There are also some good books by anointed teachers available to give you direction. One is *The Kingdom of the Cults* by Reverend Walter Martin. Reverend Bob Larson has written several books that deal with the New Age, Satanism, and cults including *Straight Answers on the New Age, Satanism, The Seduction of America's Youth*, and *In the Name of Satan*.

Jesus Christ is the eternal Son of God. He is not merely the God of this planet, but Creator and God of *all* creation. St Paul said false doctrines can lead you to "another Jesus" and "another spirit."

> **You happily put up with whatever anyone tells you, even if they preach a different Jesus than the one we preach, or a different kind of Spirit than the one you received, or a different kind of gospel than the one you believed.**
>
> **2 Corinthians 11:4 NLT**

But only one Jesus can get you into Heaven and that is the Jesus who died on the cross and bodily rose from the dead. He is Jesus Christ, God's Son!

CHAPTER 23

TAKE CARE OF YOUR BODY

God created mankind as a trichotomy. That means that you are a "little" trinity. You are made up of a spirit, a soul, and a body.

The spirit of man is fed by the Word of God. The soul is in the area of the mind and emotions. It too, must be fed a healthy diet in order to be kept in tiptop shape. We human beings are interrelated with ourselves. In other words, our spiritual life will affect our mental life and possibly our physical life. In the same way, our mental life, if it is poor, can adversely affect our spiritual lives as well as our physical bodies.

Preachers always tell people to take care of their spiritual lives, but sometimes we forget that taking care of our physical bodies is also a part of genuine Christianity. If you are born again, your physical body not only houses your personal spirit but also has become the abode of the Holy Spirit. God himself is actually living inside your body!

You surely know that your body is a temple where the Holy Spirit lives. The Spirit is in you and is a gift from God. You are no longer your own.

1 Corinthians 6:19 CEV

Therefore, you will want to take care of your body. Watch your diet! In America it has been discovered that we eat way too much sugar and salt. Some doctors believe this contributes to the high rates of cancer. Learn to regulate your diet. Stay away from foods you know are bad for you.

If you smoke or chew tobacco, ask God to deliver you from it. Believe him for the full, complete victory over any damaging habits.

Take care of the body you are living in. Follow a healthy diet and get regular exercise. You will feel better, look better, think better, and most likely live longer!

> [16] **All of you surely know that you are God's temple and that his Spirit lives in you.**
>
> [17] **Together you are God's holy temple, and God will destroy anyone who destroys his temple.**

1 Corinthians 3:16–17 CEV

> [1] **I beseech you therefore, brethren, by the mercies of God, that ye present your bodies a living sacrifice, holy, acceptable unto God, which is your reasonable service.**
>
> [2] **And be not conformed to this world: but be ye transformed by the renewing of your mind, that ye may prove what is that good, and acceptable, and perfect, will of God.**
>
> [3] **For I say, through the grace given unto me, to every man that is among you, not to think of himself more highly than he ought to think; but to think soberly, according as God hath dealt to every man the measure of faith.**

Romans 12:1–3

24

PRESS TOWARD
THESE GOALS

In general, keep these goals in mind as you seek to grow and strengthen your faith and walk in God's grace and mercy.

1. Mature as a Christian

Study your Bible and always seek to learn more about true faith. Take classes and read books by godly authors that will encourage you in your growth and development.

2. Develop a Christ-like character

In Galatians 5:22, you read about the "fruit of the Spirit," which are love, joy, peace, long-suffering, gentleness, goodness, faith, meekness, and temperance. If you make an effort to develop these qualities in yourself—with the help of the Holy Spirit—you will find yourself "growing" a Christ-like character.

3. Seek training as a worker/leader

Prepare yourself as an excellent laborer for Christ. Offer to take responsibility in your church. Find a ministry and give your best to it.

25
CHAPTER

SEEK TO DEVELOP
THESE TRAITS

As an extension of your constant efforts to grow in your faith, focus on these traits will yield great results:

- A strong prayer life
- Love for spending time in reading your Bible
- Dependability
- Loyalty to your church and faithfulness in your attendance
- Respect for leadership
- Continual deepening of your spiritual life
- An active life of Christian service
- Yielding to God's will
- A vision for world evangelism
- A heart for worship and praise
- A growing love for all people

26
CHAPTER

READ UPLIFTING MATERIAL

The Bible says to "renew your mind." You have been programmed to think like the world, and it may take a while to reprogram your thinking. But you can speed the process by reading good, well-balanced Christian material. You can ask your pastor, he or she will be able to help you in selecting good study materials.

TOOLS THAT WILL HELP YOU STUDY THE BIBLE

- **Dictionary**
- **Bible Dictionary**
- **Parallel Bible**
- **Concordance**
- **Different translations of the Bible**

You will find referring to different translations of the Bible during your study time will help you to better understand what you are reading. You will love the ***Contemporary English***

Version (CEV); the *New Life Translation* (NLT); *Amplified Bible* (AMP); and *The Message* (MSG). These are just some of the translations of God's Holy Word that are available to you.

- **Study guides, CDs, credible Christian web-sites, and podcasts**

Ask your pastor for his or her recommendations. You will find an enormous amount of resources are available on the internet as well. I use **BibleGateway.com** every day. This site includes many versions of the Bible and search features that will help you pursue your studies.

- **Books by Christian writers**
- **There are many Christian growth resources available at www.davewilliams.com**

SPECIAL PROJECTS

1. Look up the definitions of the words below:

   - Atonement
   - Conversion
   - Doctrine
   - Faith
   - Meditation
   - Prayer
   - Repentance
   - Salvation
   - Sin
   - Satan
   - Temptation
   - Worldly

2. Take a piece of paper and list the 26 things you will want to do now that you are a Christian.

CONCLUSION

There you have them. Twenty-six powerful principles and practices that will help catapult you to growth and success now that you've been given a fresh new life in Jesus. I cannot possibly emphasize enough the importance of reading God's Word daily.

You're going to have fun reading through the Bible over and over again. As you do, your faith will grow and you'll find yourself coming into a deeper, more fruitful fellowship with God. You'll discover yourself talking to others about what you've read and learned. Sooner or later, they too will want the new life you've discovered.

Don't get discouraged if there are portions of the Bible that you don't quite understand. Trust that the Holy Spirit will eventually give you understanding. As you mature, the Holy Spirit will give more revelation and light. Simply read the Bible every day and apply the principles that speak to your heart. The Holy Spirit will continue to reveal something important to you every day. It's your task to read. As you read, think of things to pray about also. Read and talk to God as you go. Ask him questions, trusting that he will answer them in time. Ask him to help you in those areas where you are weak, as the Holy Spirit reveals them to you.

Are you ready to start reading the Bible? Are you willing to read some portion each day? Are you going to place a high priority on this—before watching television or other worldly distractions? If you answered "YES!" to these questions, then I know you are destined to be a very fruitful and precious person in the new life!

About Dave Williams, D.Min.

America's Pacesetting Life Coach™

Dave is a popular speaker at rallies, minister's conferences, churches, civic group meetings, business training sessions, colleges, camps and Bible Schools. He coaches church leaders, business leaders, entrepreneurs, and followers of Christ on how to live a pacesetting life. His three-pronged approach—spiritual, attitudinal, and practical—has transformed ordinary people into extraordinarily successful leaders in every field of endeavor.

Through cultivating the individual's inherent gifts and enhancing professional—or ministry—performance, he helps to instill the kind of authentic values that attract success. He emphasizes that staying connected to the Great Commission will ultimately lead to greater levels of accomplishment.

BEST SELLING AUTHOR

Dave has authored over 60 books that teach and inspire readers in Christian growth, financial success, health and healing, and many other areas of Christian living. His book *The New Life...The Start of Something Wonderful* has sold over 2.5 million copies and has been translated into eight languages. More recently, he wrote *The World Beyond* (over 100,000 copies sold). His *Miracle Results of Fasting* (Harrison House

Publishers) was an Amazon.com five-star top seller for two years in a row. Dave's articles and reviews have appeared in national magazines such as *Advance, Pentecostal Evangel, Charisma, Ministry Today, Lansing Magazine, Detroit Free Press, World News*, and others.

PASTORAL MINISTRY

Dave Williams served as pastor of Mount Hope Church in Lansing, Michigan, for more than thirty years. In that time, Dave trained thousands of ministers through the Mount Hope Bible Training Institute, Dave Williams' Church Planter's School, and Dave Williams' School for Pacesetting Church Leaders.

With the help of his staff and partners, Dave established a 72-acre campus with worship center, Bible Training Institute, children's center, Global Prayer Center, Valley of Blessing, Gilead Healing Center, care facilities, event center, café, fitness center, world evangelism headquarters, Global Communications Center, and an office complex with nine buildings.

Church planting and missions have been a focus for Dave Williams. Under his leadership, 43 new Mount Hope Churches were planted in the United States, over 300 in West Africa, South Africa, Zimbabwe, and 200 in Asia with a combined membership exceeding 80,000 people. During Dave's tenure, Mount Hope Church gave over $40,000,000 to world and local missions.

Today, Dave serves as the global ambassador and "Bishop" for Mount Hope Churches. He also leads Strategic Global Mission (for charitable scholarships and grants), Dave Williams Ministries, Club 52 (for business people and entrepreneurs).

Dave served as a national general presbyter for the Assemblies of God, assistant district superintendent, executive presbyter, regent for North Central Bible College (now North Central University), and as a national missions board member.

Contact Information

Dave Williams Ministries
P.O. Box 80825
Lansing, MI 48908-0825

More information about Dr. Dave Williams visit:
DaveWilliams.com

Or phone:
800-888-7284
or
517-731-0000

For a complete list of Dave Williams' life-changing
books, audio messages and videos visit:
DecapolisPublishing.com

PACESETTING PRODUCTS
TO ACCELERATE YOUR SUCCESS

The Miracle of Faith Goals

This book reveals God's Plan for accomplishing great things. You will learn the seven "Vs", incremental steps, that will help you accomplish 100 to 1000 times more!

135 PAGES

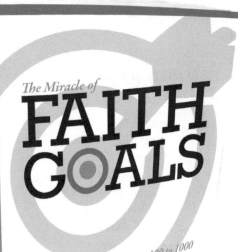

Your Spectacular Mind

Your thoughts create your environment. If you want a better life, you need better thinking. In this book, Dave Williams unlocks the mysteries of the mind, giving you plans and strategies for developing your mind—an awesome gift from God.

108 PAGES

How to Help Your Pastor Succeed

In over 30 years of successful ministry, Dave Williams has developed proven methods to assist you in helping your pastor and church succeed. You will learn: how to move to the inner circle, enforce Christ's victory in your city, spot and discern wolves, and many other strategies for supporting your pastor.

PN8038—197 PAGES

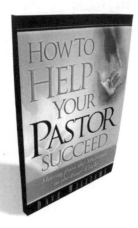

Private Garden
Tender Prophetic Words to Encourage You

In over 30 years of successful ministry. Dave Williams has experienced both triumphs and trials. But at all times—and in all circumstances—the Holy Spirit has been faithful to comfort and sustain him.

220 PAGES

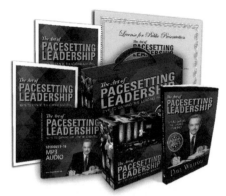

The Art of Pacesetting Leadership

In this course, you will learn the proven principles of leadership that will launch your life, ministry, business, or job to higher levels of success. Join Dr. Dave Williams on a journey of discovery as he shares the secrets of developing the heart of an authentic leader.

COMPLETE COURSE INCLUDES: 16 SESSIONS ON DVD, 16 AUDIO RECORDINGS, HARDCOVER BOOK, STUDENT MANUAL, MODERATOR'S MANUAL, & LICENSE FOR UNLIMITED PUBLIC VIEWING.

CD Sets

Creating Your New Reality

8 MESSAGES

Your Spectacular Mind

2 MESSAGES

Supernatural Gifts of the Holy Spirit

4 MESSAGES

Ebooks

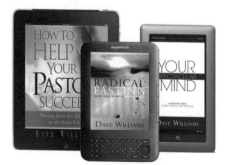

Kindle, Nook, and iBooks

Many titles are available for your e-reader!

- ° Skill For Battle
- ° The Imposter
- ° Road to Radical Riches
- ° Upward
- ° And more!

Check your ebook store for prices and easy downloads.

Certificate of Achievement

This is to certify that

_____

Having read this book, *The New Life...The Start of Something Wonderful,* and having diligently looked up all the prescribed Scripture Meditations, is hereby awarded this certificate.

On this _____ day of _____

_____
Pastor

_____
Church

The New Life…The Start of Something Wonderful

Free eBook

Visit Davewilliams.com/NL for your **FREE** ebook download

The New Life

This book will lead you through twenty-six powerful principles and practices that will help catapult you to growth and success now that you've been given a fresh new life in Jesus!

95 PAGES

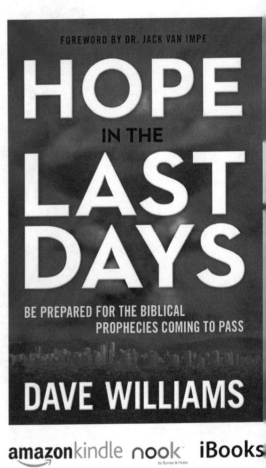